GOLDEN RETRIEVERS

KATIE LAJINESS

Big Buddy Books
An Imprint of Abdo Publishing
abdopublishing.com

BIG BUDDY DOGS

abdopublishing.com

Published by Abdo Publishing, a division of ABDO, PO Box 398166, Minneapolis, Minnesota 55439.
Copyright © 2018 by Abdo Consulting Group, Inc. International copyrights reserved in all countries.
No part of this book may be reproduced in any form without written permission from the publisher.
Big Buddy Books™ is a trademark and logo of Abdo Publishing.

Printed in the United States of America, North Mankato, Minnesota.
092017
012018

Cover Photo: Getty Images.
Interior Photos: ASSOCIATED PRESS (p. 11); Getty Images (pp. 7, 9, 13, 15, 17, 19, 21, 23, 25, 27, 29, 30); Pacific Press/Alamy Stock Photo (p. 5).

Coordinating Series Editor: Tamara L. Britton
Contributing Editor: Jill Roesler
Graphic Design: Jenny Christensen

Publisher's Cataloging-in-Publication Data

Names: Lajiness, Katie, author.
Title: Golden retrievers / by Katie Lajiness.
Description: Minneapolis, Minnesota : Abdo Publishing, 2018. | Series: Big buddy dogs |
     Includes online resources and index.
Identifiers: LCCN 2017943929 | ISBN 9781532112102 (lib.bdg.) | ISBN 9781614799177 (ebook)
Subjects: LCSH: Golden retriever--Juvenile literature. | Dogs--Juvenile literature.
Classification: DDC 636.752--dc23
LC record available at https://lccn.loc.gov/2017943929

CONTENTS

A POPULAR BREED

Dogs are popular pets. Today, Americans own more than 78 million! Around the world, there are more than 400 dog **breeds**.

One of these is the golden retriever. Let's learn why the golden retriever is the third-most popular breed in the United States.

In 2017, a golden retriever won third in the Sporting Group at the Westminster Kennel Club Dog Show.

THE DOG FAMILY

Dogs come in all shapes and sizes. Yet all dogs belong to the **Canidae** family. The name comes from the Latin word for dog, which is *canis*. This family includes coyotes, foxes, wolves, and more.

Humans and dogs have lived together for at least 16,000 years. In the beginning, humans **bred** them to hunt. Soon, they trained dogs to do other jobs such as guarding property and herding livestock.

Dogs use their bodies to communicate with humans. Movement and facial expressions help dogs share how they're feeling.

GOLDEN RETRIEVERS

The golden retriever has been a popular **breed** for more than 150 years. During the 1860s, Lord Tweedmouth of Scotland wanted a dog that could swim and **retrieve** birds.

So, he bred Tweed water spaniels with long-haired Irish setters. This produced four yellow puppies that were skilled retrievers and very handsome.

The American Kennel Club includes the golden retriever in the Sporting Group. Sporting dogs have excellent hunting skills.

Lord Tweedmouth **bred** the dogs for many years. In the end, he had long-haired dogs that could both hunt and swim. These were the first golden retrievers.

The breed came to the United States during the 1890s. In 1925, golden retrievers joined the **American Kennel Club**.

Goldens were mainly considered hunting dogs until the 1970s. That is when President Gerald Ford and his family raised a golden retriever as a pet.

President Ford had a golden retriever named Liberty. She had puppies while in the White House!

11

WHAT THEY'RE LIKE

The golden retriever makes a great pet. They are smart and kind dogs. Sometimes, goldens have service jobs. Guide dogs help blind people do daily tasks such as crossing a street.

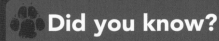
Did you know?

A golden holds the record for loudest bark at more than 113 decibels. This is as loud as a chain saw.

Search-and-rescue dogs look for people who are lost or in danger. The dogs use their sense of smell to find them.

COAT AND COLOR

Golden retrievers have a double coat. The outer coat is almost **waterproof**. Long, feathered hair covers the neck, thighs, tail, and legs.

A thick undercoat has shorter, smoother hair. It keeps the dog warm. A golden retriever's coat can range from reddish gold to nearly white.

Golden retriever puppies have short, soft coats. As they grow older, their hair gets longer.

SIZE

Golden retrievers are large dogs. On average, they stand 23 to 24 inches (58 to 61 cm) tall at the shoulder. Adult males weigh 65 to 75 pounds (29 to 34 kg). Females are somewhat smaller.

Golden retrievers look friendly and kind. They have warm, brown eyes. Their long ears are soft and silky.

Golden retrievers have black or brown noses. Cold weather can cause their noses to lighten to pink.

FEEDING

All dogs need food and water to supply energy. Quality dog food provides important **nutrients**.

Dogs can eat moist, semimoist, and dry foods. Puppies eat three or more small meals a day. Adult dogs eat one to two times a day.

Dogs should eat the same number of calories every day. Free feeding can make a dog become overweight.

CARE

Dogs require a lot of care. Golden retrievers need regular brushing to keep their coats healthy. Sometimes, they need a bath to help keep them clean. A dog should have its nails trimmed once a month. It should also have its ears checked to avoid **infection**.

Did you know?

Dogs should have their teeth brushed regularly. Like humans, brushing helps keep a dog's mouth free from infection.

Dogs should not have more than one bath each month. Too much washing with soap can leave their skin dry and itchy.

All dogs need a good veterinarian. The vet can provide health exams and **vaccines** for a golden retriever. He or she can also **spay** or **neuter** a dog.

Puppies will need to see the vet several times during their first few months. Adult dogs should visit the vet once a year for a checkup.

Some golden retrievers have hip problems. This can cause pain when walking. Vets suggest controlling a dog's weight to ease hip pain.

Every dog needs a collar with identification tags. A **microchip** can also keep a pet safe. This way, an owner can find the dog if it gets lost.

At home, a crate offers a golden a place to rest. It can also help with housebreaking puppies.

Goldens require daily exercise. If they have too much energy, they may begin unwanted chewing.

PUPPIES

A golden retriever mother is **pregnant** for about 63 days. Then, she gives birth to a **litter** of five to ten puppies.

All golden retriever puppies are born blind and deaf. After two weeks, they can see and hear. At three weeks, the puppies take their first steps.

Did you know?

Newborn golden retrievers often weigh about a pound (0.45 kg).

As they grow, golden retriever puppies change color. Their coats become the color of their ears.

THINGS THEY NEED

At eight to 12 weeks old, golden retriever puppies are ready for **adoption**. When the puppy comes home, an owner should begin obedience training as soon as it is settled.

Puppies like to be active. So, they need daily exercise and training. A golden will be a loving companion for 12 to 14 years.

The average puppy sleeps
15 to 20 hours a day.

GLOSSARY

adoption the process of taking responsibility for a pet.

American Kennel Club (AKC) an organization that studies and promotes interest in purebred dogs.

breed a group of animals sharing the same appearance and features. To breed is to produce animals by mating.

Canidae (KAN-uh-dee) the scientific Latin name for the dog family. Members of this family are called canids. They include wolves, jackals, foxes, coyotes, and domestic dogs.

infection (ihn-FEHK-shuhn) the causing of an unhealthy condition by something harmful, such as bacteria.

litter all of the puppies born at one time to a mother dog.

microchip an electronic circuit placed under an animal's skin. A microchip contains identifying information that can be read by a scanner.

neuter (NOO-tuhr) to remove a male animal's reproductive glands.

nutrient (NOO-tree-uhnt) something found in food that living beings take in to live and grow.

pregnant having one or more babies growing within the body.

retrieve to find and bring back.

spay to remove a female animal's reproductive organs.

vaccine (vak-SEEN) a shot given to prevent illness or disease.

waterproof not allowing water to pass through.

ONLINE RESOURCES

Booklinks
NONFICTION NETWORK
FREE! ONLINE NONFICTION RESOURCES

To learn more about golden retrievers, visit **abdobooklinks.com**. These links are routinely monitored and updated to provide the most current information available.

INDEX